Advanced Presentation®

_____

with

Microsoft® PowerPoint

ICDL Professional®

Conor Jordan

Conor Jordan

This edition published 2022

Copyright © Conor Jordan 2022

E-mail: conorjordan@gmail.com

Web: www.digidiscover.com

ISBN : 978-1-7396547-2-6

The intent of this manual is to provide a guide for readers to help them understand the advanced word processing and the features associated with using Microsoft PowerPoint®.

Conor Jordan does not guarantee readers will pass their respective exams because of reading this book. Its purpose is to enable readers to better understand the application that may or may not help them achieve their desired results in exams.

Revision sections are for practice purposes only and are not official ICDL tests. Sample tests for each module can be downloaded from the ICDL website to prepare students for their exams.

This book aims to give readers a clear understanding of the advanced features of Microsoft PowerPoint. It aims to achieve this by providing a step-by-step guide describing the skills needed to use this application effectively.

Downloading Resources

Resources associated with this book provide the opportunity to practice the techniques outlined. This will save the learner time to focus on the practical exercises. Visit www.digidiscover.com/downloads and click on the manual you are using.

Files should be saved in an ICDL Professional folder in 'Documents' on your computer.

Introduction

ICDL Professional is a series of digital skills modules developed to improve learners' employment prospects, capability, and competency and build on their existing knowledge. Subjects covered include advanced word processing, management spreadsheets, financial spreadsheets, advanced presentation, and advanced database. Learners can add to their learner profile using any combination of completed modules tailored to suit their workplace requirements.

The advanced modules, formally known as Advanced ECDL, which covered Microsoft Word, Excel, PowerPoint, and Access applications, have become part of the ICDL Professional series of computer modules. There are now fifteen separate modules, with a new e-commerce module soon becoming available.

The presentation guidance covered in this book may help readers develop their understanding of advanced Microsoft PowerPoint features and may prepare readers for their Advanced Presentation exam. Successful completion of this module can be added to their ICDL Professional learner profile.

For this book, it is recommended you have access to Microsoft PowerPoint 2016 or later as many of the core features described and illustrations used to involve the latest Microsoft 365 PowerPoint application using Windows on a PC. Many new additions to Microsoft PowerPoint include cloud-based services such as OneDrive and newly added Ribbon display options. For this book, the core components covered in the Advanced Presentation exam can be used with earlier versions of Microsoft PowerPoint.

When I began learning advanced presentation, I often spent long moments scanning the groups, tabs, ribbons, and different buttons on-screen, searching for the correct function. I was familiar with the software's layout but struggled to use its less obvious features. The practical aspects of the application evaded me, and I became frustrated and disheartened. It was acquiring the skills and knowledge I needed to perform tasks effectively proved to be a long, laborious endeavour.

As I became familiar with its many advanced features, I found a more straightforward way of learning. Understand what I was doing, why it was necessary, and examples of how I might apply it to real-life situations. This is why I have written this book. I hope to share my knowledge with readers that may help them improve their existing skills using Microsoft PowerPoint.

It may seem daunting at first, but learn steps one at a time. If parts prove difficult, take note of it and move on, reviewing it later with a new perspective. I hope you find this book helpful and that you progress towards using Microsoft's other applications, including Word, Excel, and Access.

Microsoft PowerPoint is available for PC and Mac. Many of the practical exercises outlined in this book are for Windows PC users. Mac users may find some of the steps, tools, dialog boxes, and features have different names or are positioned elsewhere on the screen. If you encounter any tools with other names on a Mac, it may require some time to search for them. The basic functionality is the same. It may be displayed on-screen elsewhere.

Microsoft PowerPoint is used to create slideshows enabling speakers to deliver presentations to a wide range of audiences. Independent sole traders, entrepreneurs, administrative staff, managers, and retailers are just some of the business users of Microsoft PowerPoint. Advanced presentation skills allow readers to build on their current understanding of the application, enhance their career prospects, and make performing repetitive tasks easier and more efficient.

Students can also benefit from learning advanced presentation techniques. Whether they want to improve their knowledge of presentation delivery or slideshow design acquiring the necessary skills required to do this is provided in this book.

How to use this book

I have divided the book into eight parts, each one containing a number of easily navigable sections:

Advanced Presentation will introduce you to:

Section 1 – Presentation Planning. This section guides you in preparing to deliver a presentation, including audience demographics; room layout; audio and video equipment; and slideshow design, content, and appearance.

Section 2 – Slide Masters and Templates. Here, you will discover how to maintain a consistent format, layout, and design of selected slides in a presentation. You will learn to apply the creation, formatting, modifying, and reusing of templates.

Section 3 – Graphical Objects. This section explains the tools and features you can use to create, edit, format, and position drawn objects on slides. You will learn image manipulation, object positioning, and accessibility features such as the use of alternative text.

Section 4 – Charts and Diagrams. Here, we will discuss how to represent information using charts and diagrams. You will learn how to adjust chart elements such as vertical axis formats, data labels, and legends, including topics such as flowcharts and organisational hierarchies.

Section 5 – Multimedia. This section will cover how to incorporate images, audio, video, and animated text. You will learn helpful features such as audio and screen recording, using online videos in slideshows, and background audio in a presentation.

Section 6 – Linking and Embedding. Here, you will find out how to form links between slides, images, and objects in slideshows, placing, editing, and removing embedded objects such as images, charts, and videos.

Section 7 – Importing and Exporting. Merging presentations, slides, and documents into slideshows are the topics of this section. Discover how to save slides as images and apply password protection to presentations.

Section 8 – Managing Presentations. Learn how to apply slideshow setup settings such as displaying slides without animation, options to advance slides automatically or manually, and loop shows. This section also covers important factors for presentation delivery, such as appropriate body language and gestures, storytelling, and vocal projection.

Contents

Section 1
Presentation Planning

In this section, you will learn:

- Adapt presentations to different audiences

- Technical requirements including audio and video equipment

- Design, content, and layout considerations

Considerations

PowerPoint is a versatile presentation graphics application that allows you to create stylish presentations. This application can allow you to create a range of appealing slideshows for various audiences and purposes. When creating a slideshow, there are some considerations to acknowledge. Preparation is key when delivering a presentation.

You must consider the audience before creating a presentation. The age, educational level, occupations, and cultural background of the audience will influence the slideshow's content. Ensure that the presentation is suitable for the people who will attend. For example, a presentation designed for teenagers would not be appropriate for a corporate audience.

Presentation content aims toward what the audience knows and what they can understand. It means providing a presentation that meets the audience's needs and is suited to the expected knowledge of attendees. For example, a presentation for younger students would be inappropriate for university students as they may not fully comprehend the presentation's content.

Having adequate lighting for the room is essential. Appropriate lighting is vital for an effective presentation, ensuring that the room is fit for its purpose. Poor lighting can result in difficulties viewing slides and presents a communication barrier between you and the audience.

If the room is large, you may need a microphone and a projector. It is important to project your voice around the room and ensure audience members can view the slideshow. Without a microphone, attendees towards the back of the room may not hear you clearly, resulting in confusion and loss of interest. Without a projector, the slideshow's content may not be viewable. Therefore, consider these reminders before setting up for a presentation.

The layout is essential to consider as everyone in the audience needs to see the presentation. Consider the following questions before deciding on the layout of the room. Where will the slides be displayed? Will the speaker stand front and centre before the audience or to the side? Where will the speaker position themselves, considering the audience? These factors are essential before delivering a presentation, ensuring audience members can view each slide and hear the important points in a presentation.

Ensure that the presentation's content is legible on each slide and that images, charts, videos, and text meet the audience's expectations. It is essential to have suitable video equipment so that slides can be seen clearly by everyone in the audience. Inadequate video equipment can result in poorly displayed slides and confuse audience members.

Having adequate audio equipment is also essential to ensure that the audience can hear the presentation. Always check the suitability of the audio equipment before commencing the presentation. Otherwise, members of the audience may not hear the presentation.

You can use slideshow accessories to deliver a convincing presentation. Laser pointers can emphasise important points on a slide. For example, whenever an important statistic is in a chart, a laser pointer draws attention to this essential point.

Remote clickers are another accessory used to deliver a presentation. This device allows you to progress through each slide seamlessly without having to return to the computer when advancing slides. It also allows you to return to previous slides.

Having appropriate computer display adapters can be helpful when delivering presentations in different rooms. Ensure you have the necessary adapters as connections to use a computer with a projector vary depending on the available equipment.

Ensure that you allow plenty of time to prepare before each presentation. Review slideshow material thoroughly before delivering a presentation to ensure that you can give the audience a clear understanding of what you intend to say.

There are features within PowerPoint that allow you to set a predefined time for each slide. As you are practising the delivery of the presentation, PowerPoint can record the length of time each slide will need on screen. This timing allows the presenter to deliver the presentation without manually advancing through each slide.

Design, Content and Layout

Before you create your presentation, consider the length of your slideshow. Too short, and there may not be enough time to cover all the material. Too long, and you risk of boring your audience. Plan how long you will spend delivering the presentation and what would be appropriate for the slideshow type.

Allow adequate time to display each slide so that the audience can understand and follow the information. Going through slides too quickly may make the content in a presentation too difficult to comprehend. It could make it seem as if you rush the presentation, and audience members may miss important key points in the slideshow. Go too slowly, and the audience could lose interest. Spend time practising a presentation to find the appropriate length required for each slide.

Ensure you have accompanying graphical objects included in the slideshow, such as photographs, charts, tables, or diagrams. It can help to reinforce learning and allow audience members to understand the presentation better. It can help you explain the presentation's content clearly and display information in a format audience members can understand. Graphical objects can also provide colour and variety to your presentation, making it appealing to audience members.

Apply colour combinations in your presentations to make text appear clearer. Adequate contrast makes the text stand out more, making the presentation easier to read. Avoid colour combinations that make it difficult for people to view the slideshow. Some audience members may be colour blind or have visual impairments, so providing a clear and appropriate colour set for each slide improves accessibility.

Maintain a balance between text and colour to make the content understandable and interesting. Avoid having too much colour and too many accompanying images or animations in the presentation. It may distract from the content contained within a slideshow. Increasing the size of fonts can also enable people with visual impairments to read the text in the presentation.

Alternative text describes what images or objects are in a slideshow. Alternative text allows the screen reader to describe an image, object, diagram, or graph for people with visual impairments.

Keep the level of detail concise and to the point so that the audience will comprehend the intended message of the presentation. Prolonging the length of time spent covering content in each slide can become boring for audience members, so it is important to be brief and to the point when delivering a presentation. Having cue cards will help you stick to the main points and provide the audience with a clear understanding of the presentation.

Consider providing handouts that cover the points in each slide. It can help to reinforce the material learned during the presentation. It will help audience members follow a presentation and make delivering key points easier. It can provide attendees with reference material they can then use to revise following the presentation.

Limit animations where possible so that audience members do not become distracted. Too many animations may distract from the main content, too few, and the content may become less interesting. Having a good balance between static and animated objects reduces distractions in the slideshow.

It is also helpful to include appropriate transitions to continue the presentation seamlessly and not distract audience members. With a clear understanding of advanced PowerPoint features and how to deliver content, good presentations are possible for anyone expected to give them.

Revision Section 1

1. What will influence the content of your presentation?

2. Why is a presentation suited to a particular audience?

3. What physical considerations are necessary before delivering a presentation?

4. How does room size affect the equipment used?

5. How does layout influence the delivery of a presentation?

6. What accessories help deliver a presentation?

7. What factors are considered when creating a slideshow in PowerPoint?

8. How should text and images be displayed in a presentation?

9. How should detail be provided in a slideshow?

10. What do you need to consider about animations?

Summary
Presentation Planning

In this section, you have learned how to:

- Audience demographic considerations including age, educational level, and background

- Appropriate audio equipment for room layout and video equipment for presentation clarity

- The use of colours and contrast, font styles and accompanying images for viewing

Section 2

Slide Masters & Templates

In this section, you will learn:

- Create, edit, and modify slide master layouts

- Develop and format slide master elements

- Design, adjust, and save slideshow templates

Insert a New Slide Master

Slide Masters contain formatting, objects and text that appear on each slide in a presentation. When using a slide master, the layout of all the other slides will be affected. For instance, if you include an image on the master slide, every slide in a presentation will contain that image.

1. Open the **Quarterly Report** slideshow

2. On the **View** tab in the **Master Views** group, select **Slide Master**

3. On the **Slide Master** tab, select **Insert Slide Master**

4. It will create a new **Slide Master** that you can edit to give the presentation a consistent style

5. On the **Slide Master** tab, select **Themes**, and choose **Ion Boardroom**

6. A consistent layout applies to the master slide set

7. Select **Master Layout** and click on **Slide Number**

8. It removes the slide number from each slide

9. Save the slideshow as **Master** and keep it open

Edit Slide Master Layouts

You can edit slide master layouts whenever a title, text, graphical object, or font style needs to be changed. Without adjusting every slide individually, the slide master can allow you to edit the appearance of a slideshow. It can save time when you want each slide to appear similar throughout the presentation.

1. With the **Master** slideshow open, select the third slide **Title and Content** layout

2. Highlight the first **Bulleted List Level** with the text **Click to edit Master text styles**

3. On the **Home** tab, select **Bullets** and choose **Bullets and Numbering**

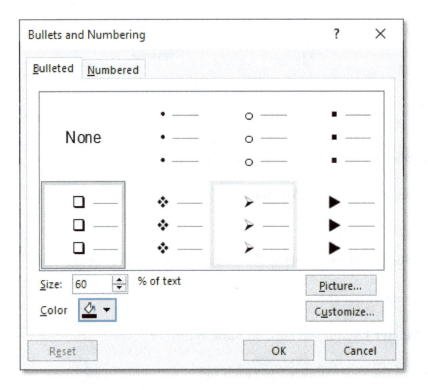

4. On the **Bullets** tab, select a **Hollow Square** style

5. Choose a **Black** colour and a **Size** of 60% of text

6. Click **OK**

7. On the **Slide Master** tab in the **Background** group, select **Background Styles** and choose **Format Background**

8. On the **Format Background** pane, choose a **Solid Fill** of **Purple Accent 6 Darker 50%** to apply to the slideshow

9. Select the **Title** and on the **Home** tab in the **Paragraph** group, **Centre** the text

10. Select the **Title Slide Layout** on the **Slide Master Pane**

11. Delete the **Footer** and the **Date** on the right of the slide by pressing the **Delete** key

12. Select the **Custom Design Slide Master** layout marked as number **2** and **Delete** it by right-clicking on it and selecting **Delete Master**

13. On the **Slide Master** tab, click on **Close Master View**

14. On the **Home** tab in the **Slides** group, select **Layout** and choose the **Ion Boardroom** slide design

15. Select slide 2

16. On the **Home** tab in the **Slides** group, select **Layout** and choose the **Ion Boardroom** slide design

17. Select slide 3

18. Apply the **Ion Boardroom** slide design

19. Save the slideshow and keep it open

Custom Slide Master

You can customise slide master layouts depending on the requirements of a slideshow. Elements such as titles, graphics, lists and images can change the appearance in a custom slide master layout. It applies a consistent style to the slideshow on each slide.

1. With the **Quarterly Report** slideshow open, click on the **View** tab

2. In the **Master Views** group, select **Slide Master**

3. Scroll down to the bottom of the **Slide Master Pane**

4. Select the final slide **Vertical Title and Text Layout**

5. On the **Slide Master** tab, select **Insert Layout**

6. It will insert a **Custom Slide Layout** at the end of the slide master pane

7. On the **Slide Master** tab, select the downward arrow to the right of **Insert Placeholder** and choose **Content**

8. Click and drag a rectangle to create a **Content** textbox

9. Centre the **Content** textbox using the **Guidelines** to extend its width equal to that of the heading

10. On the **Home** tab, change the **Font Colour** of the title text to **Black 48pt Arial**

11. Click and drag the **Custom Slide** to the second position behind the **Title Slide Layout**

12. On the **View** tab, select **Normal**

13. Select the second slide

14. On the **Home** tab in the **Slides** group, select **Layout** and choose **Custom Layout**

15. It has applied the **Custom Layout** to the second slide

16. Save the slideshow as **Custom Layout**

Creating a Template

A template allows you to apply a set design and layout to several slideshows. This template is reusable when required. For instance, if you regularly deliver a quarterly presentation on financial projections, a template saves time when preparing a slideshow.

1. With the **Custom Layout** slideshow open, on the **View** tab, select **Slide Master**

2. On the **Slide Master** tab, in the **Background** group, select **Colours** and choose the **Aspect** colour palette

3. Return to **Normal** view

4. On the **File** tab, select **Save As,** then **Browse**

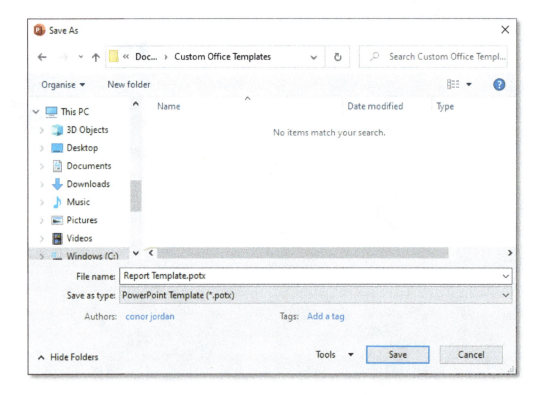

5. In the **File** Name textbox, enter the name **Report Template**

6. For **Save As Type,** choose **PowerPoint Template.potx**

7. Click **Save** and close the slideshow

Modify a Template

A template can be formatted and designed to accommodate your needs and requirements. Whenever a font type or the layout needs to be adjusted, templates can be modified so that the appearance of the template remains consistent.

1. Open **PowerPoint** and select **New**

2. At the top under **Custom** select **Custom Office Templates**

3. Select **Report Template**

4. Click on **Create**

5. Open the slideshow in **Slide Master View**

6. Select the third slide in the **Slide Master Pane** named **Custom Layout**

7. On the **Insert** tab in the Images group, select **Insert Picture From** and choose **This Device**

8. Navigate to the work files folder and select **Desk.jpeg**

9. On the **Picture Format** tab in the **Size** group, adjust the **Height** of the image to **6.07m**

10. Position the image to the right of the **Title Box**

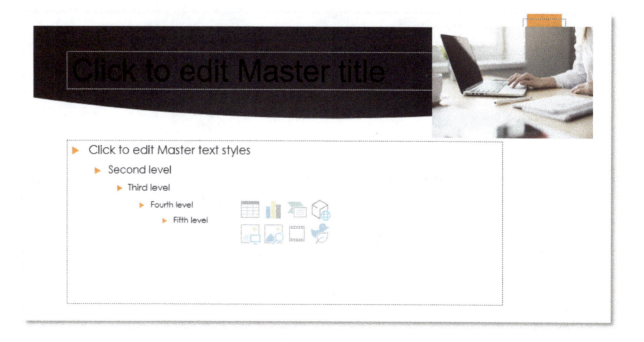

11. On the **Slide Master** tab, select **Close Master View**

12. Display slide two and notice the image positioned on the slide

13. Create a new **Custom Layout** slide

14. Each **Title and Content** slide has the image placed in the top right-hand corner

15. On the **File** tab **Save As** and choose **Browse**

16. Save the template as **Report Template**

17. Click **Save**

18. Select **Yes** to replace the template

19. It has modified the template

20. Close the slideshow and PowerPoint

Revision Section 2

1. Open the slideshow **Microsoft Office**

2. Using **Slide Master View, Insert** the **mouse.jpg** image onto the top right of each slide in the presentation

3. Edit each level of bulleted points so it displays a **Times New Roman** font and has **White Star Bullets**

4. Create a custom layout that contains a title to the top-left hand corner of the screen and content beneath

5. Change the **Colour Theme** of the presentation to a **Blue Green** colour

6. Save the slideshow as a template called **New Courses**

7. Edit the template "New Courses" so that all bulleted lists have a font of **Arial** and a **Checkmark** bulleted lists

8. Save the modified template

9. Save the slideshow as **Office Edited**

Summary

Slide Masters & Templates

In this section, you have learned how to:

- Applying consistent styles to slides using the slide master feature
- Modify, reposition, and adjust slide master elements, including titles, content boxes and images
- Saving and reusing slideshow templates

Section 3
Graphical Objects

In this section, you will learn:

- Formatting drawn objects

- Image manipulation and positioning

- Using design features in slideshows

Format Shape

Drawn shapes in PowerPoint can be formatted using various styles and colours. Objects can be rotated, coloured, and shaded using different settings. PowerPoint allows you to apply a range of formatting styles to objects. For example, you may want to include a semi-transparent rectangle with the text of a contrasting colour for a title. You can achieve this by drawing a rectangle and adjusting its opacity.

1. Open a new blank presentation

2. On the **Home** tab, select **Layout**

3. Select **Title Only**

4. Give the first slide a title of **Drawing**

5. On the **Insert** tab in the **Illustrations** group, select **Shapes** and choose **Right Arrow** under **Block Arrows**

6. Click and drag to create the **Right Arrow** shape

7. Right-click on the shape and choose **Format Shape**

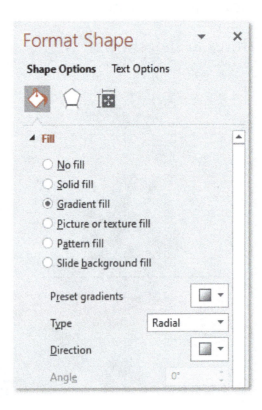

8. On the **Format Shape** pane, select **Gradient Fill**

9. Change the **Type** to **Radial**

10. Choose **Direction** of **From Centre**

11. Click on the left **Colour Gradient Stop** and select **White**

12. Click on the right **Colour Gradient Stops** and drag them to the **Right**

13. Change the colour to **Green Accent 6 Lighter 40%**

14. It applies a fill effect to the drawn object

15. Save the slideshow as **Drawing** and leave it open

Shape Transparency

You can adjust the transparency of an object to suit the style of a slide. Applying shape transparency to an object will allow other elements on a slide, such as text, to appear within the shape. Shape transparency designs a slideshow with shapes filled with text or other objects. It can also be applied when drawing shapes around images.

1. With the **Drawing** slideshow open, change the **Shape Fill** to a **Solid Fill**

2. Change the colour to **White**

3. On the **Format Shape** pane, increase the **Transparency** to **60%**

4. On the **Insert** tab in the **Text** group, select **Text Box**

5. Type in **Drawing** and centre it

6. Format the **Font** to **Arial 24pt**

7. The text is visible within the shape

8. On the **Format Shape** pane, increase the **Transparency** to **30%**

9. Notice the effect this has on the shape fill

10. Save the presentation as **Shape**

3-D Effects

3-dimensional effects apply to shapes in a slideshow. You may adjust the direction of 3D shapes to suit the style of a slide. For instance, you can adjust a right-hand facing arrow so it rotates three-dimensionally, appearing to be facing out from the screen. 3D effects apply when a presenter wants to get creative with a slideshow and include some new designs.

1. With the **Shape** slideshow open, select the right-facing arrow

2. On the **Shape Format** tab, select the **Shape Effects** icon

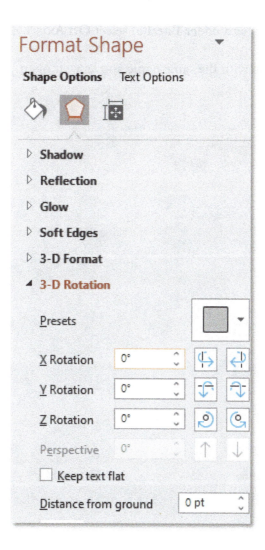

3. Choose **3D Rotation** and select the **Presets** shape to the right of the **Format Shape** pane

4. Under **Parallel** select **Isometric Left Down**

5. Apply the same **3D Rotation** to the **Drawing** textbox and position it within the right-facing arrow

6. On the **Shape Format** tab, select **Shape Effects**

7. Choose **3D Rotation** and under **Parallel** select **Off Axis 1 Right**

8. Save the presentation with the same name and leave it open

Format Painter

The format painter allows you to apply the formatting of one object to other objects. Simply copy the formatting of one object and apply it to another with the format painter.

1. Open the **Drawing** slideshow

2. Change the layout of the first slide to **Title Only**

3. Change the title to **Shapes** and **Centre** it

4. On the **Insert** tab in the Illustrations group, select **Shapes** and choose a **Cube** under **Basic Shapes**

5. Click and drag while holding down the **Shift** key to create a **Cube** shape that is proportional to its original size

6. Right-click on the shape and choose **Format Shape**

7. Choose a **Solid Fill Colour** of **Red**

8. Under **Line** choose **Solid Line** with a colour of **Black**

9. On the **Insert** tab in the **Illustrations** group, select **Shapes** and choose a **Cylinder** under **Basic Shapes**

10. Click and drag while holding down the **Shift** key to create the proportional **Cylinder** shape

11. Right-click on the **Cylinder** and choose **Format Shape**

12. Choose a **Solid Fill Colour** of **Green Accent 2 Lighter 80%**

13. Under **Line** choose **Solid Line** with a colour of **Black** and a **Transparency** of **60%**

Shapes

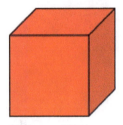  

14. Select the **Cube**

15. On the **Home** tab in the Clipboard group, select **Format Painter**

16. Click on the **Cylinder**

17. The formatting of the **Cube** applies to the **Cylinder**

18. On the **Home** tab in the Clipboard group, select **Format Painter**

19. Click on the **Cylinder**

20. Select the **Arrow**

21. The format applies to the arrow

22. Select the **Drawing** text

23. On the **Format Shape** pane under **Line**, choose a **Solid Line Colour** of **Red**

Shapes

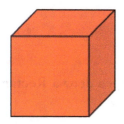  

24. On the **Insert** tab in the Illustrations group, select **Shapes** and choose an **Isosceles Triangle** under **Basic Shapes**

25. On the **Home** tab, select **Format Painter**

26. Click on the triangle

27. The same formatting applies to the triangle

28. Select the triangle

29. Delete the triangle from the slideshow using the **Backspace** key

30. Save the slideshow as **Format Painter**

Default Formatting

Default formatting allows you to draw new objects using a similar format. You can use this to draw shapes similar to a selected shape.

1. With the **Format Painter** slideshow open, right-click on the **Cube**

2. Select **Set As Default Shape**

3. On the **Insert** tab, in the **Illustrations** group, under **Basic Shapes** draw a **Rectangle: Beveled**

4. The formatting applied to the default shape is applied to any other drawn shape

5. On the **Insert** tab, in the **Illustrations** group, under **Basic Shapes** draw a **Frame**

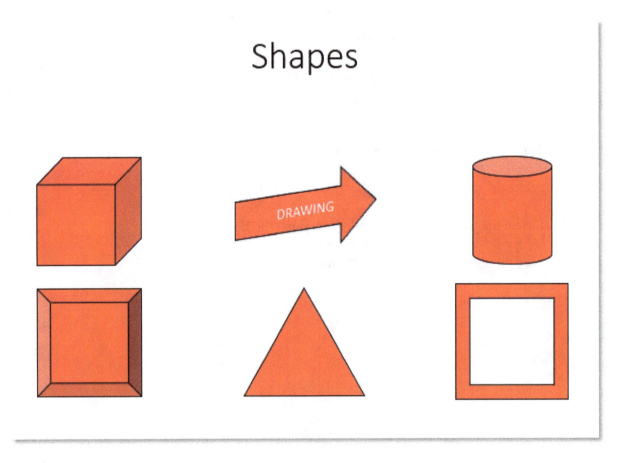

6. Save the slideshow with the same name

Image Brightness & Contrast

You can adjust images to make them appear brighter or darker. Contrast also changes the appearance of objects in a slideshow. This type of formatting changes the appearance of images to make them clearer within a presentation.

1. Open the slideshow **Team Meeting**

2. On the **Insert** tab in the **Images** group, select **Pictures** and choose **This Device**

3. Select the **Meeting.jpg** image from the work files folder

4. Place the image on the first slide to the right of the title

5. Right-click on the image and choose **Format Picture**

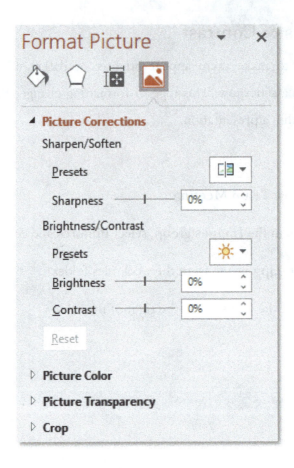

6. On the **Picture Format** tab, select **Picture Corrections**

7. Change the **Brightness** to +20% and the **Contrast** to -40%

8. On the **Picture Format** tab, select **Corrections**

9. Change the **Sharpness** to 20%

10. It adjusts the level of visible detail in the image

11. Save the slideshow as **Team Image** and leave it open

Image Colour

The colour of an image can be adjusted using PowerPoint's built-in colour saturation and colour tone tools. Colour saturation adjusts the colour intensity of an image to be increased or reduced to suit the image. It is also possible to recolour images in a slideshow to make pictures appear brighter, more colourful, or shaded. The recolour tool can completely alter the appearance of an image, and you have a range of recolour settings applicable to images in each slide.

1. Open the **Team Image** slideshow

2. With the image selected, on the **Picture Format** tab in the Adjust group, choose Picture Colour

3. Select **Grayscale**

4. With the image selected, on the **Picture Format** tab in the **Adjust** group, select **Colour**

5. Select **Black & White 50%**

6. The image colour changes to black and white

7. With the image selected, on the **Picture Format** tab in the **Adjust** group, select **Colour**

8. Select **Washout**

9. With the image selected, on the **Picture Format** tab in the **Adjust** group, select **Colour**

10. In the **Recolour** group, select **Green Accent Colour 6 Light**

11. Choose **No Recolour** to restore the colour to the original picture

12. Notice the effect this has on the image

13. Save the slideshow with the same name and leave it open

Ruler, Grid & Guides

PowerPoint has a ruler that measures dimensions in a slideshow. It is a helpful feature as it allows you to resize text, images, and objects to fit into a presentation. There are also options to use gridlines to align images and text according to your needs. Guides provide a useful tool to organise objects neatly on a slide.

1. With the **Team Image** slideshow open, on the **View** tab, select the **Ruler** checkbox

2. Adjust the position of the image so that it is 9cm to the right (A small vertical line will appear as a guide on the ruler)

3. Ensure the line represented by the image's position aligns to the right of the number on the ruler

4. Resize the image and position it so that it is 2cm towards the top and 13cm to the right

5. On the **View** tab, select the **Ruler** checkbox to hide the ruler

6. On the **View** tab, select the **Guides** checkbox to show **Guides**

7. Click and drag the **Guides** so that the top of the title text box is aligned

8. Notice how the image snaps into position next to the title

9. Reposition the **Vertical** guide to be 8cm to the right

10. Reposition the **Horizontal** guide to be 5cm towards the top

11. Position the image so that it is aligned to the top and left sides alongside the guides:

12. Select it again to hide **Guides**

13. Save the slideshow as **Guides** and leave it open

Reposition an Image

You can reposition images to fit the exact dimensions on a slide. Pictures align to the Top, Middle and Bottom and the Left, Centre and Right on a slide. It allows you to place an image at an exact position according to your requirements. For instance, an image can be positioned 5cm from the Top Right Corner to fit exactly at this place on the slide.

1. With the **Guides** slideshow open, right-click on the meeting.jpeg image and choose **Size and Position**

2. On the **Format Picture** pane, adjust the **Height** of the image to 5cm

3. Under **Position,** change the **Horizontal Position** to **30cm** from the **Top Left Corner**

4. Set the **Vertical Position** to -9cm

5. Choose to position it from the **Centre**

6. Set the **Horizontal Position** to 5cm

7. Choose to position it from the **Centre**

8. Set the **Vertical Position** to **0cm**

9. Choose to position it from the **Centre**

10. It places the image to the right of the title

Team Meeting

Weekly Department Discussion

11. Save the slideshow and keep it open

Alt Text

Alt Text allows people with eyesight difficulties to hear an explanation from a screen reader describing an image. The presenter hovers over a picture with the mouse pointer, and the PowerPoint application reads out a description. It is preferable to have one or two sentences as alt text to describe an image.

1. With the **Guides** slideshow open, right-click on the image and select **Edit Alt Text**

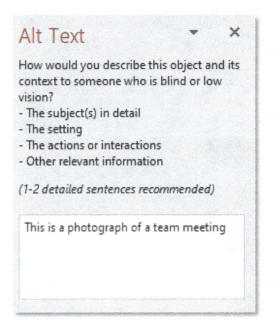

2. On the **Alt text pane**, type in "This is a photograph of a team meeting."

3. Close the **Alt Text** pane

4. Right-click on the image and select **Edit Alt Text** again

5. Edit the text that will be read by the screen reader to "This is a picture of a group meeting."

6. Use the **Backspace** key to remove the text in the **Edit Alt Text** box

7. Save the slideshow and close it

Distribute Objects

You can arrange objects horizontally or vertically on a slide. This feature saves time by distributing all objects quickly and evenly. It is useful when you have many objects on a slide and want to rearrange them to appear inline.

1. Open the slideshow **Monthly Meetings**

2. Select the speech bubble on the bottom right-hand corner of the second slide

3. On the **Home** tab in the **Drawing** group, select **Arrange** and choose **Align**

4. Select **Distribute Horizontally**

5. The speech bubble appears horizontally relative to other objects on the slide

6. Select the image on the left-hand side of the slide

7. On the **Home** tab in the **Drawing** group, select **Arrange** and choose **Align**

8. Select **Distribute Vertically**

9. The image displays vertically relative to other objects

10. Save the slideshow and leave it open

Cropping Images

Images can be reduced in size to show only a portion of the original image. It is useful when only a part of a picture is required or removing unnecessary detail in an image. You may adjust the height and width of an image to specific dimensions. For example, the cropping tool is used when you want to display only a portion of an image without showing its remainder.

1. With the **Monthly Meetings** slideshow open, select the image on the left-hand side of the second slide

2. On the **Picture Format** tab in the **Size** group, select **Crop**

3. Adjust the **Width** setting to 8cm

4. It has adjusted the height of the image in proportion to the width

5. Click and drag the **Right-Hand Side** of the **Crop Lines** to reduce the size of the image

6. Click and drag the **Left-Hand Side** until the width is 5cm

7. Click on the **Crop** button again to reduce the size of the image to the new dimensions

8. Click on the arrow below the **Crop** button and select **Aspect Ratio**

9. Choose **Portrait 3:4**

10. Click on the **Crop** button

11. The image appears with an **Aspect Ratio** of **3:4** in **Portrait**

12. Click and drag the edges of the **Crop Markings** until they fill the original image

13. Click on the arrow below the **Crop** button and select **Aspect Ratio**

14. Choose **Landscape 4:3**

15. Click on the **Crop** button

16. The image appears according to an **Aspect Ratio** of **4:3** in **Landscape**

17. Save the slideshow as **Crop**

Photo to Drawn Object

PowerPoint has a feature allowing you to convert an image to appear like a drawn object. It can be applied when you want a picture to appear as if it has been drawn or to give it an artistic feel. For example, if you have a photograph of a seaside town and want it to appear as drawn, you can apply the photo to drawn object formatting to the image.

1. With the **Crop** slideshow still open, select the image to the left of the slide

2. On the **Picture Format** tab in the Adjust group, select **Artistic Effects**

3. Select **Pencil Greyscale**

4. Right-click on the image and select **Format Picture**

5. On the **Picture Format** tab, click on the **Effects** icon

6. Under **Artistic** Effects, adjust the **Pencil Size** slider to 40

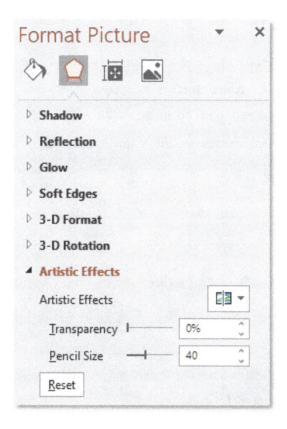

7. Select **Artistic Effects**

8. Select **Watercolour Sponge**

9. Save the slideshow and leave it open

Save Image as PNG

PNG (Portable Network Graphics) Format is a higher-quality image format. This type of image may be used on websites or edited further in image manipulation software packages. GIF (Graphics Interchange Format) applies to images with a solid colour, text, and line art. BMP (Device Independent Bitmap) images are high quality and have large file sizes. JPEG (File Interchange Format) is a high-quality image format often used in presentations and websites.

1. With the **Crop** slideshow open, right-click on the image on the second slide

2. Right-click and choose **Save As Picture**

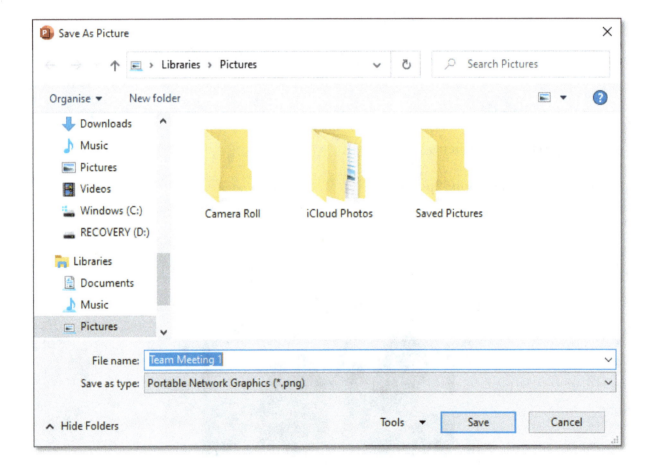

3. For **Save As Type**, choose **Portable Network Graphics (*.png)**

4. Name the image in the **Save As** textbox as **Team Meeting 1**

5. Click **Save**

6. Navigate to the work files folder on your computer

7. A **PNG** image appears in the folder

8. It opens using another image viewer application such as **Photos**

9. Return to the slide

10. Right-click and choose **Save As Picture**

11. For **Save As Type**, choose **Graphics Interchange Format (*.gif)**

12. Name the image in the **Save As** textbox as **Team Meeting 2**

13. Click **Save**

14. Navigate to the work files folder on your computer

15. A **GIF** image appears

16. It opens using another image viewer application such as **Photos**

17. Repeat the same process for saving a **Windows Bitmap (*.bmp)**

18. Save another copy of the image in **JPEG File Interchange Format (*.jpeg)**

19. Navigate to the work files folder, and you will be able to see the various formats saved,

20. Leave the slideshow open

Background Graphics

Slideshows can contain background graphics that appear on each slide. It can allow you to design a slideshow that is appealing and colourful. Depending on your requirements, you can choose to hide background graphics from selected slides or show them. For example, if you want to apply a background graphic of mountains to a slide, you can choose a picture of mountains from online photos and use the background graphics feature to apply this to the background of selected slides.

1. Open the **Monthly Meeting** slideshow

2. Right-click on a space on slide 2 of the presentation and choose **Format Background**

3. The **Format Background** pane displays

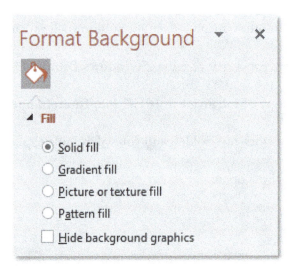

4. Deselect the **Hide Background Graphics** checkbox

5. The background graphics hide from view on the slide

6. Select the **Hide Background Graphics** checkbox again to display the background graphics

7. Select **Picture or texture fill**

8. For **Texture** select a texture fill of **Marble** from the options available

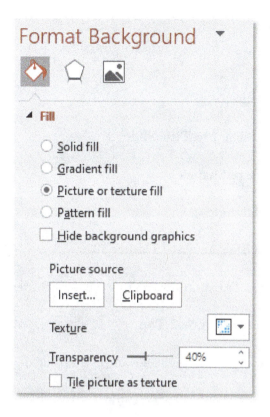

9. Deselect the **Tile picture as texture** checkbox

10. The **Marble** effect will no longer appear tiled as the background for the slide

11. Adjust the **Transparency** to 40%

12. Click on **Apply to All**

13. It will apply the **Marble** background to each slide

14. Display the first slide and notice the change in the background

15. **Undo** the change to the background by using the **Quick Access Toolbar** shortcut

16. Display the second slide and select **Reset Background** on the **Format Background** pane

17. Save the slideshow and close it

Revision Section 3

1. Create a new presentation

2. Adjust the **Layout** of slide 1 to **Title Slide**

3. Give slide one the title of **Shapes**

4. Draw an **Isosceles Triangle**

5. Apply a **Solid Fill** of **Blue Accent 1 Darker 50%**

6. Make the triangle **75% Transparent** and move it over the text

7. Apply a **3D rotation** of **Off Axis 2 Top**

8. Rotate the shape **180** degrees until the **Triangle** is upside down

9. Draw a left-facing arrow next to the **Triangle**

10. Apply a **Gradient** colour fill of **Light Gradient Accent 1**

11. Use the **Format Painter** to apply the format of the **Triangle** to the **Arrow**

12. Use **Default Formatting** to draw a **Circle** using the same formatting

13. On slide 2 of the presentation, **Insert** the **Team Meeting 3 BMP** image

14. Adjust the **Brightness to +30%** and the **Contrast to -30%**

15. Apply a **Grayscale** effect to the image

16. Use **Gridlines** to place the image in the top right-hand corner of the slide

17. Set the **Horizontal Position** of the image at **10cm** and the **Vertical Position** to **8cm** from the **Top Left Corner**

18. Remove the **Gridlines**

19. Change the **Alt Text** to "Image of a person teaching a class."

20. Return to slide one and apply a **Distribute Horizontally** setting to all shapes

21. Return to slide two and crop the image with a width of 7cm

22. Convert the image to a drawn object and save the picture in a GIF format called **Drawn Image**

23. Save the slideshow as **Colour** and close it

Summary
Graphical Objects

In this section, you have learned how to:

- Creating and formatting drawn objects such as cubes, triangles and 3D shapes

- Adjusting colour saturation, brightness, and contrast

- Using the ruler, guides, and gridlines to reposition elements on slides

Section 4

Charts & Diagrams

In this section, you will learn:

- Create, modify, and change chart types

- Formatting chart elements

- Create and adjust diagrams

Format Chart

You can format charts to display information contained within a table of data in different ways. The title, legend, data labels and chart are adjustable to suit its purpose. Depending on the information provided, formatting can be applied to a chart to display data.

1. Open the **Company Profits** slideshow

2. Select the second slide

3. On the **Insert** tab in the Illustrations group, select **Chart**

4. Choose a **Line Chart**

5. Enter the following information into the accompanying spreadsheet:

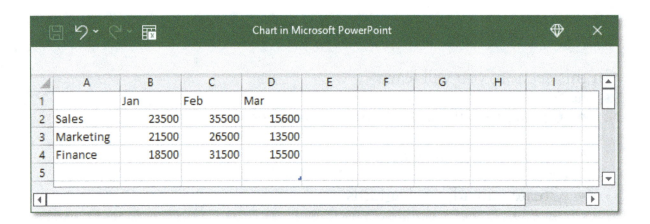

6. Change the **Chart Title** to **Sales Figures**

7. On the **Home** tab, change the **Font** to **Arial, 20pt, Bold**

8. Right-click on the **Legend** and choose **Format Legend**

9. Select **Fill & Line**

10. Choose a **Dark Green Accent 2 Darker 25%**

11. Select **Text Options** on the **Format Legend** pane

12. Choose a **Colour** of **White**

13. Click on the **Vertical Axis** to the left of the chart

14. On the **Format Axis** pane, select **Text Options**

15. Choose a **Black** colour

16. On the **Home** tab, change the **Font** to **Arial 14pt**

17. On the **Format Axis** pane, select **Axis Options**

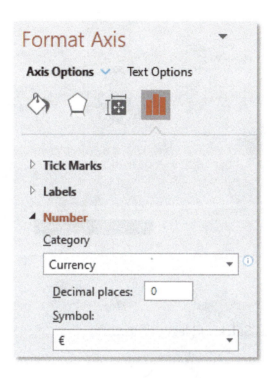

18. Scroll down to the **Number** category

19. Change **Category** to **Currency** with 0 **Decimal Places**

20. On the **Chart Design** tab in the **Charts** Layout group, select **Add Chart Element**

21. Choose **Data Labels** and **Below**

22. Select the **Data Labels** for **February**

23. On the **Format Data Labels** Pane, under **Number,** for **Category,** choose **Currency** to **0 Decimal Places**

24. Repeat the same process for **January** and **March**

25. The finished chart should look like this:

26. Save the slideshow as **Sales** and leave it open

Change Chart Type

You can change a chart to another chart type, such as a bar chart, into a line chart. The type of chart used varies depending on the information provided, the audience, and the slideshow style.

1. Open the **Sales** slideshow

2. Select the **Line** Chart on slide 2

3. On the **Chart Design** tab in the **Type** group, select **Change Chart Type**

4. Select a **Clustered Column Chart** and click **OK**

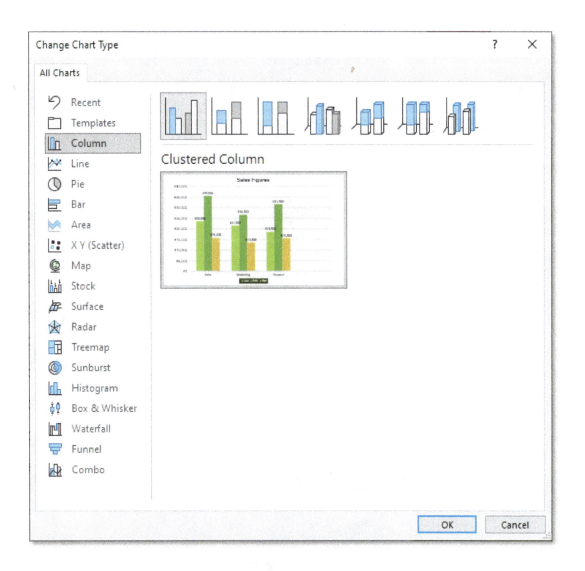

5. Click on the **January** column (Light Green)

6. On the **Format Data Series** pane, select **Series Options**

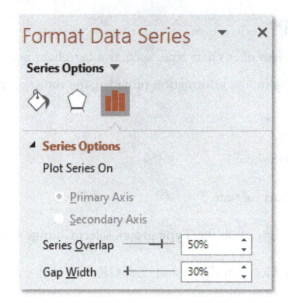

7. Adjust the **Series Overlap** slider to 50%

8. Adjust the **Gap Width** slider to 30%

9. The columns in the chart now overlap

10. Save the slideshow and leave it open

Chart Image

You may set an image as the chart background making the chart appear more interesting. You can also use pictures to represent information in a chart. For example, a computer company may want to display the total number of computers sold. A column chart containing stacked images of computers represents data in a clear way.

1. With the **Sales** slideshow still open, select a **Column** representing **February** sales

2. On the **Format Data Series** pane, select **Fill & Line**

3. Choose **Picture** or **Texture Fill**

4. Under **Picture Source,** choose **Insert**

5. Choose **From a File**

6. Select the **Ball.png** from the work files folder and click on **Insert**

7. On the **Format Data Series** pane, select **Stack**

8. Images now represent the February columns

9. Select the **Chart Area** (Chart background)

10. On the **Format Chart Area** pane, select **Fill & Line**

11. Choose **Picture or Texture Fill**

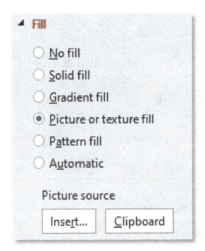

12. Under **Picture Source**, click on the **Insert** button

13. Choose **From a File**

14. Select the image **Trees.jpg** from the work files folder

15. Select **Insert**

16. On the **Format Chart Area** pane, adjust the **Transparency** to **70%**

17. Select the **Tile Picture as Texture** checkbox

18. Adjust the **Offset X** to 10pt (Along horizontal axis)

19. Adjust the **Offset Y** to -20pt (Along vertical axis)

20. Change **Scale X** to 80%

21. Change **Scale Y** to 75%

22. Select an **Alignment** of **Centre**

23. Choose a **Mirror Type** of **Horizontal**

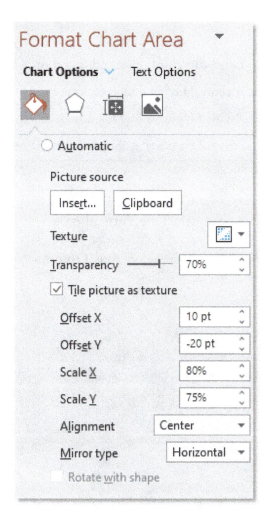

24. It formats the appearance of the **Chart Area** background

25. Save the slideshow as **Formatted Chart**

Value Axis

The scale of axis values is the range of values displayed based on a data table. Changing this will adjust how the data appears in a chart. Having a high maximum axis value will mean that the data peaks in the chart will reduce in size. Having a low maximum axis value means that this data will increase in size. You can adjust the major units in the chart to reflect this.

1. With **Formatted Chart** open, select the **Vertical Axis**

2. On the **Format Vertical Axis** pane, select **Axis Options**

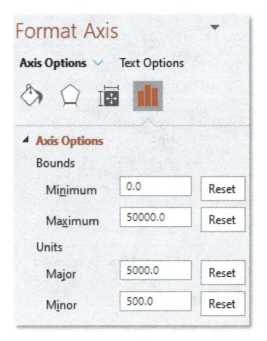

3. Under **Bounds,** change the **Minimum** Axis Value to 0.0

4. Change the **Maximum** Axis Value to 50000.0

5. Change the **Major** Units to 5000.0

6. Adjust the **Minor** units to 500.0

7. For **Display Units,** select **Thousands**

8. Depending on the values displayed in a chart, you can adjust **Display Units** to **Hundreds, Thousands** or **Millions**

9. Deselect the **Show display units label on chart**

10. It removes the **Thousands** label on the **Vertical Axis** of the chart

11. Save the slideshow and close it

Flowchart

A flowchart is a visual representation of the hierarchy within an organisation. A flowchart displays managerial positions towards the top and subordinate positions below. Positions next to each other hold the same ranking in an organisation, e.g. administrative positions.

1. Open a **Blank Slideshow**

2. Change the **Layout** of the first slide to **Title and Content**

3. Enter the title **Sales Department** and centre it

4. Select the **Content** box

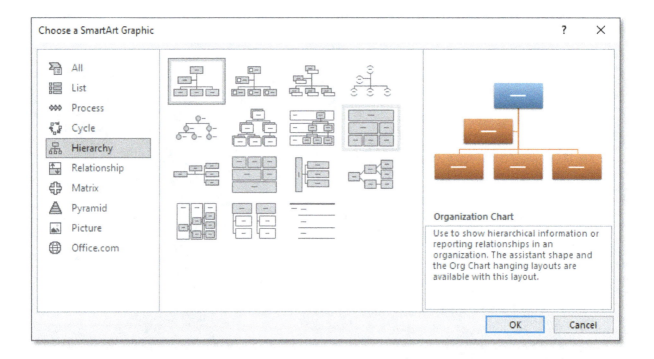

5. On the **Insert** tab in the Illustrations group, select **Smart Art** and choose **Hierarchy**

6. Select **Organisation Chart**

7. Click **OK**

8. Delete the **Shape** on the **Second Level** of the hierarchy with the **Backspace** key

9. Delete one of the **Shapes** on the **Bottom Level** of the hierarchy with the **Backspace** key

10. Fill in the following information into the flowchart:

Top Process Shape   Manager - Mary Wilson

Bottom Left Alternate Process   Supervisor - John Dunne

Bottom Right Alternate Process   Supervisor - George Mitchel

11. It has created a flowchart representing the hierarchy within the company

12. Save the slideshow as **Flowchart** and leave it open

Manipulating Shapes

You can adjust shapes to present the information in a flowchart. It is helpful to use an efficient way to represent the hierarchy within an organization or department. You can change the connections between objects in a flowchart to suit the style of the flowchart.

1. Open the **Flowchart** slideshow

2. Select the **Supervisor – John Dunne** shape

3. On the **SmartArt Design** tab in the **Create Graphic** group, select the arrow beside the **Add Shape** button and select **Add Shape After**

4. Select the shape and on the **SmartArt Design** tab in the **Create Graphic** group, select **Text Pane**

5. Include the title of **Sales Assistant Fiona Jones** for the new shape

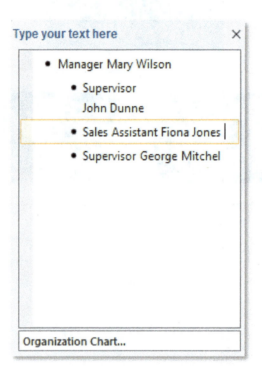

6. Close the **Text Pane**

7. On the **SmartArt Design** tab in the **Create Graphic** group, select **Demote**

8. It has demoted the **Sales Assistant**

9. On the **SmartArt Design** tab, in the **Create Graphic** group, select **Right to Left**

10. **Fiona Jones** is now a subordinate to the **Supervisor John Dunne**

11. Select the **Manager Mary Wilson**

12. On the **SmartArt Design** tab, in the **Create Graphic** group, select the arrow beside the **Add Shape** button and choose **Add Assistant**

13. Right-click on the blank shape and select **Edit Text**

14. Type in **Personal Assistant – Michael Smith**

15. Select the shape representing **George Mitchel**

16. On the **SmartArt Design** tab, in the **Create Graphic** group, select the arrow beside the **Add Shape** button and select **Add Shape Below**

17. Right-click on the shape and choose **Edit Text**

18. Enter **Sales Assistant – Mark Breen**

19. Select the entire organisational chart

20. On the **SmartArt Design** tab, in the **Create Graphic** group, select **Layout** and choose **Standard**

21. Change the **Font** to **Bold** for each position in the hierarchy

22. The **Organisation Hierarchy** should look like this:

23. Create a **Title and Content** slide for slide 2

24. In the middle of the content section, select **Insert a SmartArt Graphic**

25. Under **Cycle** select **Basic Cycle**

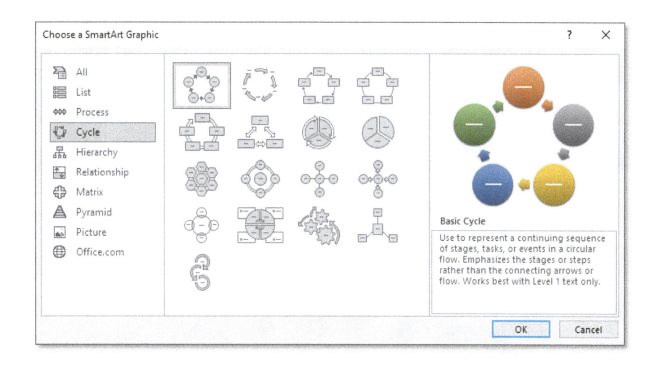

26. Click **OK**

27. Enter a title of **Teamwork** and **Centre** it on the slide

28. Enter the following terms:

i.   Co-operation

ii.   Communication

iii.   Collaboration

iv.   Networking

v.   Sharing

29. On the **SmartArt Design** tab in the **SmartArt Styles** group, select **Change Colours** and choose **Colourful – Accent Colours**

30. To the right of **Change Colours,** select the downward arrow to choose a **Fill** and under **3D** select **Flat Scene**

31. Click and drag the **Content Box** to enlarge the **Basic Cycle**

32. The finished slide should look like this:

33. Create a **Title and Content** slide for slide 4

34. In the middle of the content section, select **Insert Smart Graphic**

35. Under **Pyramid,** select **Basic Pyramid**

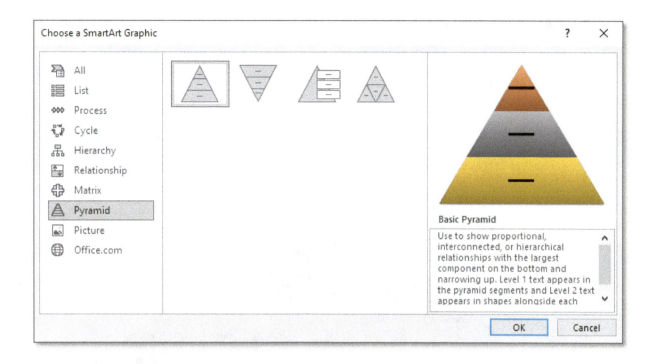

36. Click **OK**

37. Enter a title of **Objectives** and centre it

38. Enter the following terms:

i.   Results

ii.   Productivity

iii. Morale

39. On the **SmartArt Design** tab in the **SmartArt Styles** group, select **Change Colours** and choose **Colourful Range – Accent Colours 4 to 5**

40. Under **3D** select **Inset** for the **Fill**

41. Adjust the **Font** for **Results** to **30pt**

42. The complete **Pyramid** should look like this:

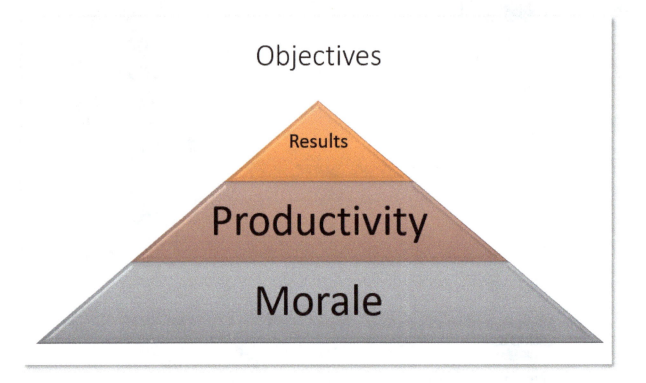

43. Save the slideshow as **Sales Department** and close it

Revision Section 4

1. Open a **Blank Presentation**

2. Insert a **Bar Chart** with the **Default** values and enter a title of **Sales Figures**

3. Change the chart title font to **Arial 24pt Bold**

4. Format the legend to have a **Solid Fill of Black Text 1 Lighter 50%** colour and a **White** font colour

5. Change the chart type to a **Column Chart**

6. Adjust the **Gap Width** slider to **20%**

7. Adjust the **Series Overlap** to **40%**

8. Apply a **Gradient Fill** of **Light Gradient 6** to the **Chart Area**

9. Insert the image record.png and apply a **Stack** format for the **Series 1** column

10. Change the **Major Units** on the **Vertical Axis** to **1.5**

11. On a new slide, create a **Flowchart** showing the **Department Hierarchy** for the following employees:

i.   Manager – Mary Dunne

ii.   Supervisor – Michael Hughes

iii.   Supervisor – John Daly

iv.   Employee (Subordinate to John Daly) – Sarah Walsh

12. Save the presentation as **Sales Team**

Summary

Charts & Diagrams

In this section, you have learned how to:

- Inserting column, bar, line, pie and combo charts to represent information

- Applying formatting to data labels, vertical axes, legends and chart areas

- Designing diagrams including flowcharts and organisational hierarchies

Section 5

Multimedia

In this section, you will learn:

- Include audio and video in slideshows

- Use screen and audio recording in presentations

- Applying animation effects to text, images and charts

Insert Online Video

Videos can accompany a presentation to explain a topic further or visually represent information for the audience. You can insert online videos into a slideshow from websites such as YouTube. Any video that has a URL plays in a slideshow.

1. Open the **Media** slideshow

2. Ensure that you connect to the internet

3. Display the second slide

4. On the **Insert** tab in the **Media** group, select **Video**

5. Choose **Online Video**

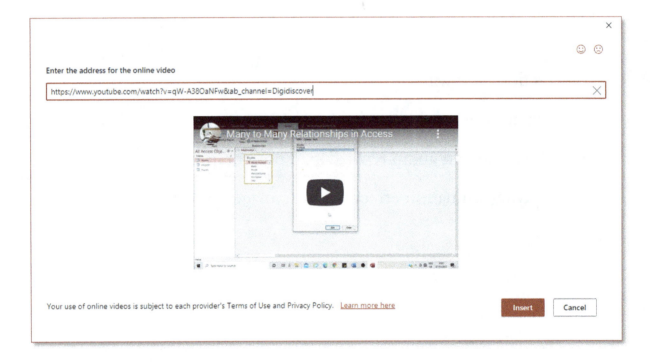

6. Enter the YouTube URL for the **Many-to-Many Relationships in Microsoft Access:**

   https://www.youtube.com/watch?v=qW-A38OaNFw&ab_channel=Digidiscover

7. Click on **Insert**

8. On the **Video Format** tab in the **Video Styles** group, select **Bevelled Frame, Gradient**

9. On the **Playback** tab in the **Video Options** group after **Start,** choose **Automatically**

10. On the **Playback** tab in the **Preview** group, select **Play**

11. Preview the slideshow

12. End the slideshow

13. On the **Playback** tab in the **Video Options** group after **Start,** choose **When Clicked On**

14. Preview the slideshow

15. Click on the video to play it

16. End the slideshow

17. Save the slideshow as **Media** and leave it open

Inserting Audio

Audio may describe graphics or charts to reinforce the message conveyed in a presentation. You can include audio in a slideshow to provide the audience with accompanying information. Audio can play in the background while a speaker gives a presentation. The sound plays when you select the speaker icon.

1. Open the **Media** slideshow

2. Display the third slide

3. On the **Insert** tab in the **Media** group

4. Choose **Audio** and select **Audio from my PC**

5. Select the **Piano.mp3** file from the work files folder

6. On the **Playback** tab in the **Audio Options** group, after **Start,** choose **Automatically**

7. Preview the slideshow

8. The audio will play when the speaker symbol is selected

9. Select the **Play Across Slides** checkbox

10. Select the **Hide During Show** checkbox

11. Preview the slideshow from the **Audio Clip** slide

12. The audio will play across the remaining slides while remaining hidden

13. On the **Playback** tab in the **Audio Options** group, after **Start,** choose **When Clicked On**

14. Save the slideshow and leave it open

Audio Recording

An audio recording can accompany a presentation to provide background information on key points in a slideshow. This feature is useful when the speaker wants to provide additional details about a subject.

1. With the **Media** slideshow open, display the fourth slide

2. On the **Insert** tab in the Media group, select **Audio**

3. Choose **Record Audio**

4. Name the Recorded Sound **Narration**

5. Allow PowerPoint access to your computer's built-in microphone or external microphone

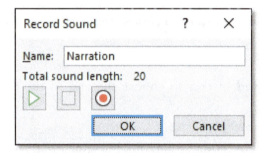

6. Click on the **Record** button and record a message describing the slideshow

7. Record twenty seconds of audio using a microphone or the built-in microphone on your computer

8. When the recording finishes, click on the **Stop** button

9. Click on the **OK** button

10. The recording appears on the slide

11. Preview the slideshow

12. When you reach the fifth slide, click on the **Play** button to play the recording

13. The recording plays back

14. On the **Playback** tab in the **Audio Options** group, select the **Rewind After Playing** checkbox

15. On the **Playback** tab in the **Editing** group, select **Trim Audio**

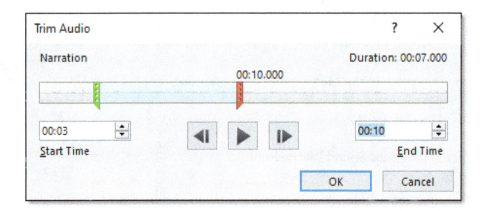

16. Click and drag the **Green** marker to choose the beginning of the audio, in this case, after one second

17. Click and drag the **Red** marker to choose the end of the audio, in this case, after two seconds

18. You may adjust the **Start Time** by entering the time into the textbox. You can also change it with the up and down arrows

19. Change the **End Time** by entering a number into the textbox. The up and down arrows also allow you to adjust the duration.

20. Click **OK**

21. Preview the slideshow and click on the speaker icon

22. The edited audio recording will play when clicked on

23. Save the slideshow and leave it open

Screen Recording

Screen recordings can be performed in PowerPoint to record any activity on the screen of your computer. The screen recording appears in a slideshow as a video. For example, if a computer teacher wants to show how to create a simple spreadsheet in Excel, these steps can be recorded using a screen recording played back in a slideshow.

1. With the **Media** slideshow open, display the fifth slide

2. On the **Insert** tab in the **Media** group, select **Screen Recording**

3. This setting prepares the application to record the slide show

4. Choose the **Select Area** button to choose what area of the screen records

5. Open **Microsoft Word**

6. Create a **New Document**

7. Click on the **Record** button

8. There will be a three-second countdown before the screen recording begins

9. Type the text "This is a screen recording" into the document

10. Click on the **Stop** button

11. The **Screen Recording** appears on the slide

12. Resize the **Screen Recording** by clicking and dragging on the edges of the video frame

13. On the **Slideshow** tab in the **Start Slide Show** group, click on **From Beginning**

14. When you reach the fifth slide, **Play** the **Screen Recording**

15. End the slideshow

16. On the **Slideshow** tab in the **Start Slide Show** group, click on **From Beginning**

17. Hover the mouse pointer over the row of buttons on the bottom left of the screen

18. The **First** button displays the previous screen

19. The **Second** button displays the following screen

20. Advance to slide two by clicking on the second button

21. Click on the **Third** button

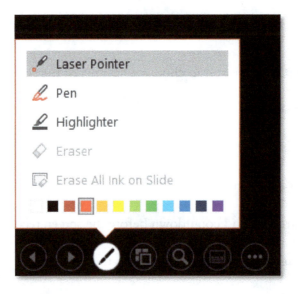

22. It provides options to use a **Laser Pointer**, **Pen**, and **Highlighter**

23. Use the **Laser Pointer** to highlight the text **Relationships in Access** on slide 2

24. Click on the **Third** button

25. Select the **Pen** option

26. Use the **Red Pen** to underline the sentence **Relationships are created between tables**

27. Advance to slide 3

28. Change the colour of the pen to **Dark Blue**

29. Circle the text **Audio clips can be inserted into a slideshow**

30. Advance to slide 4

31. Click on the **Third** button

32. Use the **Highlighter** to emphasise the text: **This can provide more information about slides in a presentation**

33. When the slideshow has finished, choose to **Discard** the **Ink Annotations**

34. Save the slideshow and leave it open

Background Audio

You may play audio recordings in the background while giving a presentation. It is a helpful feature that allows speakers to have audio play while explaining the details of a slideshow. For example, a computer teacher may want to provide background information about the history of computers and use pre-recorded background audio to explain the slideshow for this purpose.

1. With the **Media** slideshow open, display the third slide

2. Select the **Speaker** icon for the **Audio Clip**

3. On the **Playback** tab in the **Audio Styles** group, select **Play in Background**

4. On the **Playback** tab in the **Audio Options** group, click on **Volume** and select **Medium**

5. On the **Playback** tab in the **Editing** group, change the **Fade Duration** for **Fade In** to **03.00**

6. For **Fade Out,** enter **02.00**

7. It will gradually increase and decrease the volume of the audio to the set times

8. Preview the slideshow

9. The audio will play in the background as the slides advance with the **Fade In** and **Fade Out** settings applied

10. Save the slideshow

Animation Settings

Images, charts, and diagrams can have animations applied to them. You may adjust the timings of each animation to produce a range of effects for each slideshow object. It can make a presentation seem more interesting.

1. Open the slideshow **Microsoft Office**

2. Display slide 2 of the slideshow

3. On the **Animations** tab in the **Animation** group, apply a **Fade** animation to the image

4. On the **Animations** tab in the **Advanced Animations** group, click on **Animation Pane**

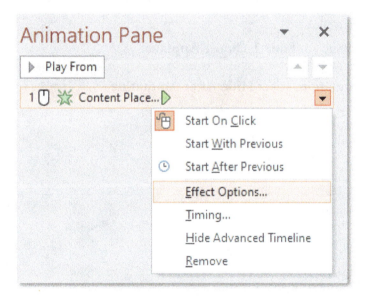

5. Click on the **Downward Facing** Arrow next to the animation and select **Effect Options**

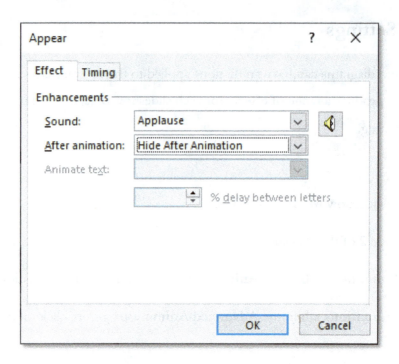

6. On the **Effect** tab for **Sound,** choose **Applause**

7. For **After Animation,** select **Hide After Animation**

8. Select the **Timing** tab

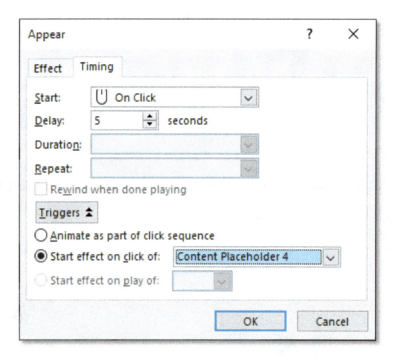

9. For **Start** choose **On Click**

10. Adjust the **Delay** to **5 seconds**

11. For **Triggers,** select **Start Effect on click of** and choose **Content Placeholder 4**

12. Click **OK**

13. It will start the effect when you click on the content placeholder

14. Preview the slideshow and notice the effects the animation has on the image

15. Save the slideshow and leave it open

Animating Bulleted Lists

Animations apply to bulleted lists to make text appear on a slide when the presenter clicks on the screen. Avoid using too many animation effects in a presentation to avoid distracting the audience from the slideshow's content.

1. Open the slideshow **Microsoft Office**

2. Display slide 3 of the slideshow

3. Select the first listed bullet point **Word**

4. In the **Advanced Animation** group, apply a **Fade** animation

5. Select the second listed bullet point **Excel**

6. In the **Advanced Animation** group, apply a **Swivel** animation

7. Select the third listed bullet point **PowerPoint**

8. In the **Advanced Animation** group, apply a **Zoom** animation

9. Select the fourth listed bullet point **Access**

10. On the **Advanced Animation** tab, apply a **Random Bars** animation

11. Select the fifth listed bullet point **Outlook**

12. On the **Advanced Animation** tab, apply a **Float In** animation

13. Select the **Word** animation and choose **Effect Options**

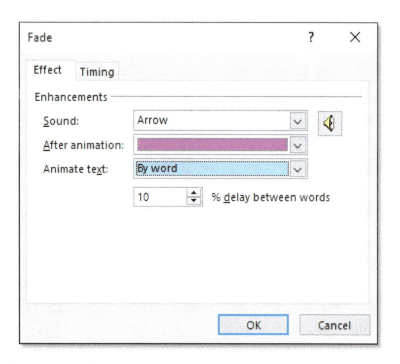

14. For **Sound**, choose **Arrow**

15. Select a **Purple** colour for **After Animation**

16. For **Animate Text** choose **By Word**

17. Choose a **10% delay between words**

18. Click **OK**

19. Right-click on the **Excel** animation on the **Animation** pane

20. Select **Timing** and for **Start** select **After Previous**

21. Click **OK**

22. Select the **PowerPoint** animation on the **Animation** pane

23. Select **Timing** and for **Start** select **With Previous**

24. Click **OK**

25. It will play the **Excel** and **PowerPoint** animations together after the **Word** animation

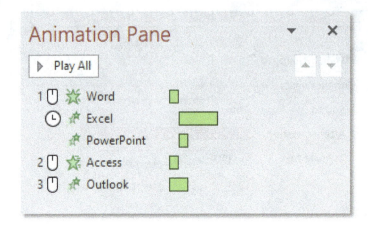

26. On the **Animation Pane**, select **Access** and click on the **Up Arrow** to move the **Access** animation to the second to be played

27. Preview the slideshow and notice the effects the animations have on each bullet point

28. Save the slideshow as **Animated** and leave it open

Animating Charts

Animations can be applied to data series, labels, axes, and elements in a chart. When you click on the slide, separate elements appear with different animations applied. Avoid using too many animation effects in a presentation to avoid distracting the audience from the slideshow's content.

1. With the **Animated** slideshow open, display slide 4

2. Highlight the **Columns** in the chart representing **Males**

3. On the **Animation** tab in the **Animations** group, click on the **Arrow** and choose **More Entrance Effects**

4. Apply a **Blinds** animation

5. Click **OK**

6.   On the **Animations** pane, select the downward-facing arrow and choose **Effect Options**

7.   On the **Chart Animation** tab, for **Group Chart,** select **By Series**

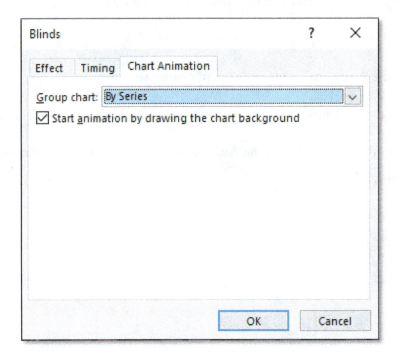

8.   Click **OK**

9.   Preview the animated chart

10. On the **Animations** pane, select the downward-facing arrow and choose **Effect Options**

11. On the **Chart Animation** tab, for **Group Chart,** select **By Category**

12. Click **OK**

13. Preview the slideshow and notice how the chart is animated by category

14. Select the **Slide Show** tab and select **Set Up Slide Show**

15. Select the **Show Without Animation** checkbox

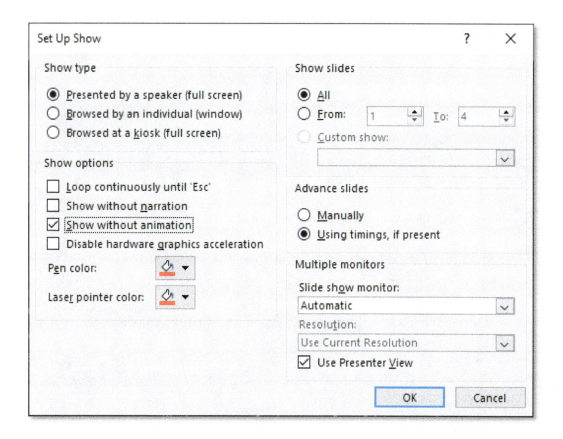

16. Click **OK**

17. Preview the slideshow

18. Notice how there are no animations in the slideshow

19. Save the slideshow and close it

Revision Section 5

1. Open the presentation **Multimedia**

2. Ensure you connect to the internet

3. Insert an online presentation with a YouTube video of your choice on slide 2

4. Insert the audio file **JazzLounge.mp3** into slide 3

5. Make an audio recording describing the Jazz Lounge audio file and place it on slide three as well

6. Make a screen recording on slide four by typing out the following list while recording:

- Project your voice

- Emphasise key points

- Use open body language

- Keep points concise and brief

7. Play the screen recording back

8. Set the **JazzLounge.mp3** audio file as the **Background Audio** to the slideshow

9. On slide 5, apply a **Fly In** animation to the shape on the left

10. Apply a **Split** animation to the shape on the right

11. Include the sound of **Applause** to accompany the animations

12. Apply an animation that turns the bulleted list text on slide 4 to white

13. Save the presentation as **Our Media**

Summary

Multimedia

In this section, you have learned how to:

- Placing audio and video into slideshows and editing playback options

- Recording audio and screen activities for presentation demonstrations

- Apply animations to text, bullet points, images and chart elements

Section 6

Linking & Embedding

In this section, you will learn:

- Linking slides and images in presentations

- Embed external files into slides

- Breaking links between external files

Action Button

Action buttons can be placed on a slide to perform different functions, such as linking to another slide in the presentation. Action buttons may apply a shortcut that advances to another slide, display a video, or play audio. The presenter clicks on the button, and the task completes.

1. Open the **Office Rules** slideshow

2. Display the first slide

3. On the **Insert** tab in the **Illustrations** group, select **Shapes**

4. Under **Action Buttons**, select **Get Information**

5. Click and drag to draw the document action button

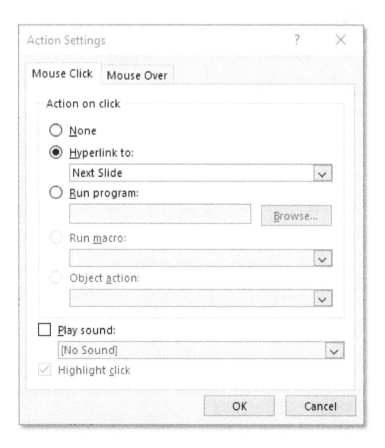

6. On the **Mouse Click** tab, select **Hyperlink to:** and choose **Next Slide**

7. Click **OK**

8. Click **OK** again

9. On the **Shape Format** tab, change the shape fill and shape outline to **White**

10. Preview the slideshow and click on the action button

11. It will bring you to the next slide

12. With the same slide open, on the **Insert** tab, select **Shape**

13. Under **Action Buttons**, select **Document**

14. On the **Mouse Click** tab, select **Link to:** and choose **URL**

15. Type in www.digidiscover.com

16. Click **OK**

17. Preview the slideshow

18. Click on the **Document** action button

19. It will bring you to the website address

20. Save the slideshow as **Linked** and leave it open

Linking Objects

You may link objects in a slideshow. When a presenter clicks on a linked object in a slideshow, it will open the file associated with that object. It is useful when the presenter wants to open a file without minimising PowerPoint and opening another application. For example, a linked Word document may be linked to a slide in a presentation so that when a presenter clicks on the icon, the document will open.

1. With the **Linked** slideshow open, display the fourth slide titled **Health and Safety**

2. On the **Insert** tab, in the **Text** group, select **Object**

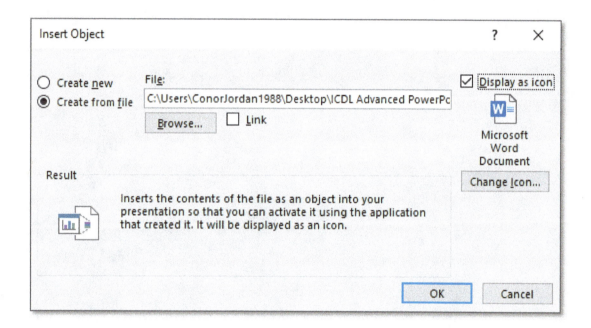

3. Select **Create From File** and click on **Browse**

4. Select the "Health and Safety" document file to place on the slide

5. Select **OK**

6. Select the **Display as Icon** checkbox

7. Click **OK**

8. Change the **Layout** of the slide to the **Title and Content** layout

9. Select the **Content** box

10. On the same slide on the **Insert** tab, select **Object**

11. Select **From File**

12. Select the **Health and Safety** Word document again

13. Select the **Link** checkbox

14. Click **OK**

15. The contents of the document appears in the content section of the slide

16. Double click on the document, and it will open in Microsoft Word

17. Save the presentation and leave it open

Updating Links

When changes apply to linked objects in a slideshow, it is possible to update these links. It is useful when you need to change files and update the linked files. For example, updating the link will be reflected in the slideshow when the content of a linked Word document is changed.

1. Open the **Health and Safety** document related to the **Linked** presentation

2. Change the fourth bullet point to read "Workers have a responsibility."

3. Save the document with the same name and close it

4. Preview the slideshow again

5. When you preview the slideshow and reach the fourth slide, the fourth bullet point will have changed

6. Save the slideshow and keep it open

Break a Link

Sometimes it is necessary to break a link with a file. It may be because the file is no longer needed or the information in the slideshow changes. For example, when the presenter no longer wants a button to open a specific document, you may remove the link. Changes to the original file will not appear in the slideshow.

1. With the **Linked** slideshow open, select the linked document on the fourth slide

2. On the **File** tab, select **Info**

3. Scroll to the bottom of the page and click on **Edit Links to Files**

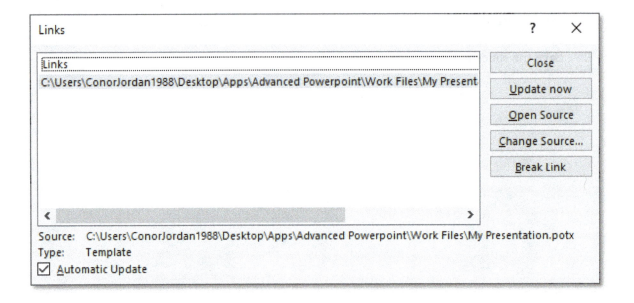

4. Click on **Break Link**

5. Select **OK**

6. When you preview the slideshow and change the contents of the document, there will no longer be a link

7. Save the slideshow and keep it open

Linked Image

Images may link to another file, application, or web page in a presentation. When a link is created for a picture, clicking on it can open a new file application or display a website.

1. Display slide 7 in the **Linked** slideshow

2. On the **Insert** tab in the **Images** group, select **Pictures**

3. Select **This Device**

4. Select the **PC.jpg image** from the work files folder and click on **Insert**

5. Resize the image to fit onto the slide

6. On the **Insert** tab in the **Links** group, select **Link,** then **Insert Link**

7. On the **Email Address** tab, enter example@mail.com as the email address

8. Include a subject of "Presentation Enquiry."

9. Click **OK**

10. Preview the slideshow

11. Click on the PC image

12. The email application on your computer will prepare an email to the example email address.

13. Save the slideshow and keep it open

Embedding an Object

Embedding objects places elements without links to another external file in the slideshow. Any changes made to the original file do not appear in the presentation. For example, when you want to insert a spreadsheet into a slideshow but do not wish to make any changes, embedding this object will place the spreadsheet in a slide without a link to the original file.

1. Display slide 8 in the **Linked** presentation

2. On the **Insert** tab in the **Text** group, select **Object**

3. Select **Create From File** and choose **Browse**

4. Locate and **Open** the **Annual Sales** spreadsheet file

5. Select **OK** and click **OK**

6. It has embedded a spreadsheet into the slide

7. Double-click on the chart

8. Change the **Sales** to 160,000

9. Preview the slideshow

10. When you make a change to the spreadsheet, this does not appear in the embedded chart

11. Open the original **Annual Sales** spreadsheet

12. The **Sales** value remains at 145,000 for the **1st Quarter**

13. Save the presentation

Edit & Delete Embedded Data

You may edit embedded objects on a slide in PowerPoint. It is useful when the presenter wants to change information within a slideshow while leaving the original file unchanged. Changes do not appear in the original file.

1. With the **Linked** presentation still open, double-click on the spreadsheet

2. The spreadsheet opens with Excel features available

3. Change the **Sales** amount in cell B3 to €120,000

4. Notice the effect this has on the chart

5. Adjust the **Expenditure** amount in cell B4 to €100,000

6. Save the workbook and close it

7. Preview the **Linked** presentation again

8. Notice that there is a change to the chart on slide 8

9. Select the spreadsheet object and press the **Backspace** key to delete it

10. Save the slideshow as **Modified** and close it

Revision Section 6

1. Open the **Journalism Studies** slideshow

2. Create an **Action Button** on slide two that acts as a **Hyperlink** to the document **Journalism**

3. Insert the **Object News Reporting** document into slide three and create a **Link**

4. Delete the first sentence in the **News Reporting** document

5. **Update** the link

6. **Break** the link

7. Insert the Books.jpg image into slide four and link it to www.digidiscover.com/books

8. **Embed** the **Balance Sheet** spreadsheet into slide 5

9. Edit cell B4 to €17,500

10. Delete the embedded spreadsheet

11. Save the slideshow and close it

Summary

Linking & Embedding

In this section, you have learned how to:

- Inserting action buttons to link slides in a presentation

- Placing unlinked images and external files such as spreadsheets and charts in slides

- Removing external links in slideshows

Section 7

Importing & Exporting

In this section, you will learn:

- Merging slides into a slideshow

- Applying password protection to presentation

- Save presentations in different file formats

Combining Presentations

You can combine two separate slideshows to create one slideshow. It can save time when both presentations are completed and need to be put together, rather than manually copying slides. For example, a sales employee may have two separate slideshows containing sales for the previous two months.

1. Open the **Computer Classes** slideshow

2. On the **Home** tab, select the arrow beside **New Slide**

3. Choose **Reuse Slides**

4. Click on **Browse** and select the **Sales Figures** slideshow and select **Open**

5. Select the **Sales Figures** slides

6. It will merge the single slide containing the chart and adjust formatting to the presentation style

7. With the **Reuse Slides** pane displayed, click on **Browse**

8. Select the **Microsoft** PowerPoint file to merge with and click **OK**

9. Right-click on the first slide and choose **Insert All Slides**

10. It includes all slides from the slideshow in the current presentation

11. Using the **Ctrl** key, select the second and third slides

12. Use the **Backspace** key to delete them

13. Preview the slideshow

14. Save the slideshow as **Merged**

Merge a Word-processed Outline

You can include Word documents into a slide in a presentation. The document needs to be in Outline view to merge with the slideshow. You may adjust the formatting of the document to suit the style of the slideshow. For example, a presenter may have a Word document to put into a slideshow. You can achieve this by merging the document with the presentation.

1. With the **Computer Classes** slideshow open, display slide five titled **Applications Covered**

2. On the **Home** tab, click on **New Slide**

3. Select **Slides From Outline**

4. Select the **Applications Covered** document and click on **Insert**

5. The **Outline** appears in the presentation

6. On the **Home** tab in the **Clipboard** group, use the **Format Painter** to copy the formatting of the slideshow to this slide

7. Save the slideshow and leave it open

Save a Slide as an Image

You can save each slide in a presentation as images in different formats such as JPEG and BMP. For example, if a computer teacher needs a copy of a slide containing a labelled PC and wants to save it as a PNG image, they can save the entire slide for future reference.

1. Open the **Merged** slideshow and display slide two titled **Sales Figures**

2. On the **File** tab, select **Save As,** then **Browse**

3. For **Save As Type,** select **JPEG**

4. Click **Save**

5. Select **Just This One**

6. Name the image **Slide**

7. It will save the slide as a **JPEG** image

8. Display slide 3 **Exams**

9. On the **File** tab, select **Export**

10. Choose **Change file Type** and select **PNG**

11. Select **Save** and choose **Just This One**

12. The slide saves as a PNG file

13. Display slide four titled **Further Your Career**

14. On the **File** tab, select **Save As,** then **Browse**

15. Name the files **Presentation**

16. For **Save As Type,** select **BMP**

17. Select **Save** and choose **All Slides**

18. Click **OK**

19. It will save each slide in a **BMP** format onto your computer

20. On the **File** tab, select **Export**

21. Choose **Create Animated GIF**

22. Select the **Make Background Transparent** checkbox

23. Adjust the **Seconds to Spend on each Slide** setting to **2**

24. Choose slides **1** to **5**

25. Select **Create GIF**

26. Name it **Animation** and select **Save**

27. Navigate towards the work files folder and notice the newly saved images

28. Follow the same steps to save the presentation and choose **RTF Rich Text Format** for the **File Format**

29. Click on **Save**

30. Export the presentation again and select the **File Format MP4 Video**

31. It will export the presentation as a video file

32. Locate the slideshow and preview it as an **MP4 Video**

33. Save the presentation and close it

Password Protection

Presenters can apply a password that is required when the slideshow opens. It means that only those with the password may open the slideshow. There is also an option to apply a password when a user wants to modify a slideshow. Only those with the password may edit the slideshow, allowing users without the password to view it without making any changes. Both passwords can be applied to a slideshow when the contents of a presentation is private.

1. With the **Merged** slideshow open, on the **File** tab, select **Save As** and select **Browse**

2. Select **Tools** and choose **General Options**

3. Under **Password to Open,** select the **Encrypt this presentation and require a password to open**

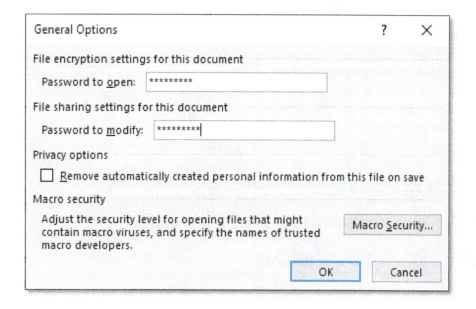

4. Enter a password of "Secret" in the **Password To Open** textbox

5. It will prompt the user to enter a password before opening a presentation

6. Enter a password of "Secret" in the **Password To Modify** textbox

7. It will allow users who do not know the password to view the presentation but save the presentation with a different name

8. Click **OK**

9. Re-enter both passwords again and save the presentation as **Passwords**

10. Close the presentation

11. Re-open the presentation

12. A prompt appears requesting you to enter a password to open the slideshow

13. You will be unable to modify the presentation until you enter the password to modify

14. You also have the option of opening the slideshow in **Read-Only** format, which allows you to view the slideshow without being able to make any changes

15. Enter the password to modify

16. You are now able to modify the slideshow

17. On the **File** tab, select **Save As** and choose **Browse**

18. Select **Tools** and choose **General Options**

19. In the **Password To Open** textbox, delete the password

20. In the **Password To Modify** textbox, delete the password

21. Save the presentation as **Password**

Revision Section 7

1. Open the **Journalism Studies** and **Media** slideshows

2. **Merge** every slide of the **Journalism Studies** slideshow with the **Media** slideshow

3. Insert slide 2 of the **Multimedia** slideshow into slide 3 of the **Journalism Studies** slideshow

4. Create a new slide at the end of the slideshow

5. **Merge** the document **Multimedia Outline** with the blank slide

6. Save the Multimedia slide of the presentation as a **BMP Image** called "Multimedia Image."

7. Apply a **Password to Open** "Classified" and a **Password to Modify** "Hidden" to the slideshow

8. Save the slideshow as **Media Studies**

Summary
Importing & Exporting

In this section, you have learned how to:

- Including slides from other presentations to create custom slideshows

- Protecting presentations with passwords to open and modify

- Saving presentations in different formats such as Rich Text Format .rtf

Section 8
Managing Presentations

In this section, you will learn:

- Apply slideshow setup settings

- Using presenter controls during a slideshow

- Presentation delivery including practice, body language and vocal projection

Creating Custom Shows

You can create a custom slideshow by including, rearranging, and saving a new presentation consisting of slides from other slideshows. It is a helpful feature that allows the presenter to create a presentation that includes essential information from different sources rather than creating a new slideshow from the beginning.

1. Open the **Our Shop** slideshow

2. On the **Slide Show** tab in the **Start Slide Show** group, select **Custom Slide Show**

3. Select **Custom Shows**

4. Click on the **New** button

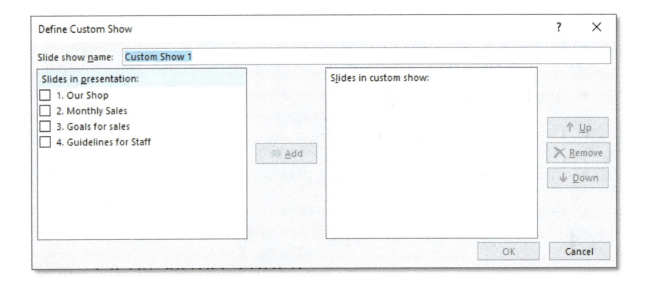

5. Select the checkboxes of the "Our Shop" and "Monthly Sales" to include in the custom show

6. Click **Add** to include the slides

7. Select the "Monthly Sales" slide in the custom show and click **Up** to move the slide up one slide

8. Click **OK**

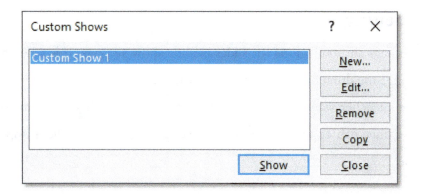

9. Click on the **Copy** button to copy the custom show

10. It will produce a copy of the show

11. Click on the **Edit** button

12. It will allow you to make changes to the slideshow

13. Change the order of slides so that the "Our Shop" title page appears first

14. Click on the **Remove** button to delete the custom show

15. Select **Close**

16. Save the slideshow as **Custom Slide Show**

Slide Show Settings

You can adjust timings and transitions for slides in slide show settings. It is a helpful feature that allows you to change the duration of each slide and the transitions that occur between slides. For example, suppose a teacher wants to deliver a presentation within the timeframe of a scheduled class. In that case, they can apply timings to each slide to ensure that slides appear within the chosen timeframe.

1. With the **Our Shop** slideshow open, display slide 1

2. On the **Slides** pane, select the first two slides by holding down the **Ctrl** key

3. On the **Transitions** tab, choose a **Fade** transition

4. In the **Timing** group, change the **Duration** of the transition to **1.50** seconds

5. Click on the **After** checkbox and choose **3.00** seconds

6. For **Sound** select **Arrow**

7. Click on **Apply To All**

8. It will apply a 1.5 second transition to all slides with an **Arrow** sound

9. Preview the slideshow

10. Select the **After** checkbox again to remove the **Advance Slide** timing

11. Save the slideshow and leave it open

Loop Shows Continuously

You can loop slideshows continuously so that when the presentation plays, it restarts from the beginning and continues until manually stopped. The presenter can then end the slideshow by pressing the **Esc** key.

1. With the **Our Shop** slideshow open, on the **Slide Show** tab, select **Set Up Slide Show**

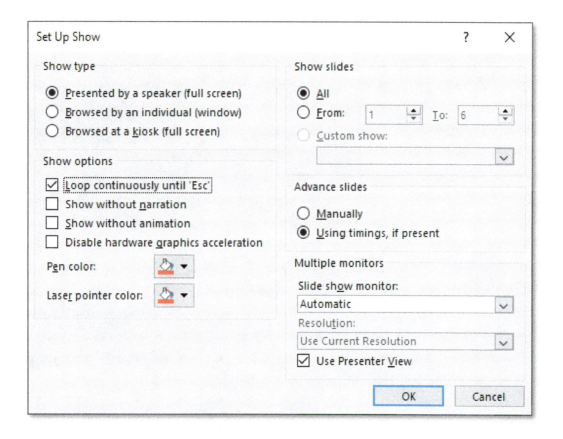

2. Select the **Loop Continuously Until Esc** checkbox

3. It will apply a continuous loop to the slideshow until you press the **Esc** button

4. Click **OK**

5. Preview the slideshow

6. It will loop continuously

7. To remove this setting, open the **Set Up Show** dialog box again and deselect the checkbox and click **OK**

8. Save the presentation

Advance Slides

There are options to advance slides manually by clicking or using a key on the keyboard. It gives the presenter control over how long each slide appears. There is another option to use set timings for each slide. Manually advancing slides allow the presenter to choose how long each slide appears in a presentation.

1. With the **Our Shop** slideshow open, open the **Set Up Show** dialog box again

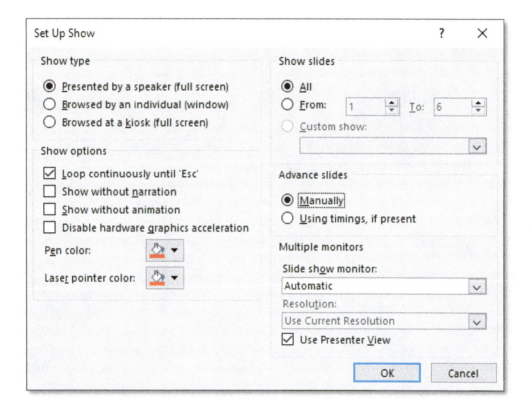

2. Under **Advance Slides**, select **Manually**

3. Click **OK**

4. Preview the slideshow

5. Slides will be advanced when you press a key or click the mouse

6. To use set timings for your presentation, open the **Set Up Show** dialog box again

7. Under **Advance Slides**, select **Using Timings, if Present**

8. Click **OK** and save the slideshow

9. Change the slide duration to **2 seconds** and **Transitions** to **1 second**

10. Preview the slideshow

11. Timings apply to the slideshow

Without Animation

The presenter can save the slideshow without any animation. Applying this setting can reduce distractions when delivering a presentation.

1. Open the **Set Up Show** dialog box again

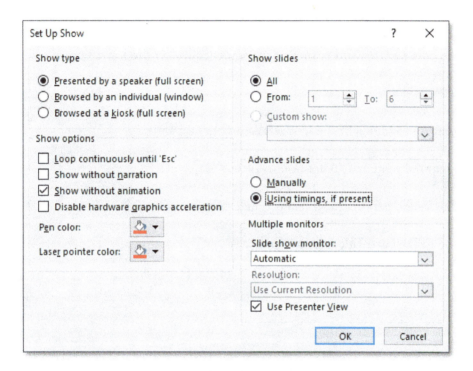

2. Under **Show Options**, select the **Show Without Animation** checkbox

3. Click **OK**

4. Preview the slideshow

5. The slide show appears without animation

6. Open the **Set Up Show** dialog box again

7. Select the **Show Without Animation** checkbox and click **OK**

8. Preview the slideshow again with animations

9. Save the presentation

Slide Show Delivery

You can use the pen feature to highlight essential points in a slideshow as it displays on the screen. It is useful when the presenter wants to emphasise key parts in a slide. You may remove markings and annotations and advance to the next slide.

1. Open the presentation **Progress Review**

2. Preview the slideshow

3. On the bottom left-hand corner of the screen, click on the **First** button on the left

4. Select **Pen**

5. Use the pen to highlight the word "Teamwork" on slide 3

6. Highlight the sentence "Attention to Detail."

7. To remove the pen marks, finish the slideshow

8. Choose to **Discard Ink Annotations**

9. Save the slideshow

Slide Show Controls

Some features allow the presenter to turn the screen white or black during a presentation. This keyboard shortcut applies when the speaker wants to draw attention away from the screen and elaborate on a point.

1. Preview the **Progress Review** slideshow

2. Press the **B** key to turn the screen **Black**

3. Press it again to return to the slideshow

4. Press the **W** key to turn the screen **White**

5. Press it again to return to the slideshow

6. Press the **S** key to stop the show

7. Press the **S** key to restart the show

8. Press **Esc** to display the **Normal** view

9. Save the slideshow and leave it open

Presenter View

The presenter view displays a different screen to the view shown to the audience. This view has controls that allow the speaker to preview slides before showing the audience. The presenter can advance slides and view the time elapsed in the presenter view.

1. Preview the **Progress Review** slideshow

2. Right-click and select **Show Presenter View**

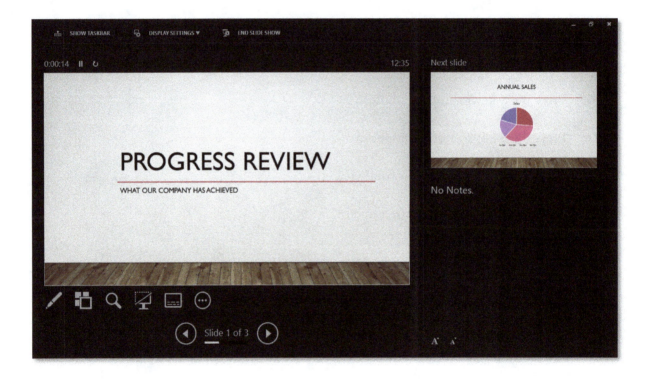

3. Slides can be selected using the slide thumbnails at the bottom of the screen

4. Click on the **Right Arrow** to advance slides and the **Left Arrow** to go to the previous slide

5. The timing of the presentation appears next to the **Pause** button above the active slide

6. Alternatively, you can use the **Arrow Keys** on the keyboard

7. Continue to the end of the slideshow

8. Save and close the presentation

Presentation Considerations

Practice

Adequate preparation is key to creating a good presentation and communicating your overall message. It is important to practice delivering a presentation before you present a slideshow. It will allow you to assess the timing of each slide and determine how it will fit in with your delivery. Rehearsing the timings of slides is essential as having slides advance for the duration of your speech will make the presentation run smoothly. You can also adjust the content to suit the audience. Design the slideshow so that it is suitable for the intended audience.

Tone of Voice

Communicate clearly by emphasising points in your presentation. Reinforce key points using an appropriate tone of voice so that the audience receives and understands the overall message. Ensure the pitch of your voice is suitable for the type of presentation you are giving. Project your voice so that audience members will be able to hear you. Consider incorporating pauses to allow the audience to comprehend the information explained.

Body Language

Use open body language and maintain good posture while delivering your presentation. Emphasise points with hand movements and gestures to reinforce the message you want to convey. Avoid using too many hand gestures and movements that may distract the audience from the slideshow. Having hunched shoulders or slouching may affect the projection of your voice, so maintaining good posture is essential.

Storytelling

Storytelling with real-life examples on an important point may improve information recall among audience members. It is a helpful technique to explain theories, statistics, or definitions. It can give the audience context by providing anecdotes or examples that apply to practical situations. Giving background information related to the main points may help attendees recall the slideshow's content.

Revision Section 8

1. Open the **Furniture Store** slideshow

2. Create a **Custom Slide Show** with the first, third and fourth slide

3. Move the third "Expected Quarterly Sales" slide up to slide 2

4. Apply a **Fade** transition to all slides with a duration of 2 seconds

5. Apply a setting that will **Loop the Show Continuously**

6. Apply a setting that **Advances Slides** automatically

7. Set up the show so that animations do not appear on the slideshow

8. Preview the slideshow and underline "Treat loyal customers with respect" with the pen

9. Erase all pen marks on the slide

10. Turn the screen white using a keyboard shortcut

11. Restore the screen

12. View the slideshow in **Presenter View**

13. Save the slideshow as **Furniture Store Plan**

14. Why is it important to practice a presentation before giving it?

15. What should your tone of voice be in terms of your presentation?

16. How should your body language be while delivering a presentation?

Summary
Managing Presentations

In this section, you have learned how to:

- Adjusting slideshow options, including looping shows continuously and without animation effects

- Using presenter controls such as turning the screen black or white and highlighting text with the pen or highlighter

- Delivering a presentation effectively with preparation, appropriate body language and vocal projection

Index

Value Axis, 65

W

Without Animation, 128

Value Axis, 65